Original title:
The Grapes of Reflection

Copyright © 2025 Creative Arts Management OÜ
All rights reserved.

Author: Sophia Kingsley
ISBN HARDBACK: 978-1-80586-229-1
ISBN PAPERBACK: 978-1-80586-701-2

Roots of Inspiration

In a garden where ideas sprout,
Some roots twist and twirl, just like a dance.
They trip on weeds, then laugh out loud,
Oh, inspiration, you're quite the prance.

Digging deep for that perfect thought,
With a spade more crooked than a turtle's shell.
The carrots giggle at their own good looks,
While the potatoes murmur, 'We age so well!'

Canvas of the Forgotten Harvest.

On canvas sprouted drinks of lore,
Forgotten fruits with faces to show.
Faded colors but tales galore,
Artists sip, hoping for an overflow.

A pear debates with a cheeky plum,
'No one remembers you, but here I shine!'
They clink their glasses, make a fun thrum,
As drinks spill stories of time divine.

Whispers of Vintage Wines

In forgotten cellars, secrets sleep,
A cabernet tells jokes that are aged.
The merlot's laughter is a sip so deep,
While a tired chardonnay feels quite caged.

Bubbles rise in a playful jest,
'La de da, we're better than tea!'
With every pour, they pass a test,
As the cork pops, it's a jubilee!

Shadows Beneath the Vines

Beneath the vines, where shadows play,
A grape decides it wants to groove.
It tumbles down, ready for the fray,
Joining the dance, it finds its move.

With giggles among the leafy scenes,
They play tag with the sun's last rays.
In this patch of cheer, no in-betweens,
Just merry wines in wild displays.

Echoes of a Harvest Moon

Under the moon, we stomp and play,
As bunches giggle at the end of the day.
With sticky toes and squishy cheer,
The juice of fun is always near.

Baskets full, we skip and glance,
The silly dance of grape romance.
Squash the fears, let laughter bloom,
In every drop, we find the room.

Secrets in a Vineyard's Heart

Whispers travel on the vine,
A grape confesses, 'Aren't we fine?'
Chasing shadows in a leafy maze,
Where every twist sparks silly gaze.

Blaring horns from birds that sing,
As grape bunches swing and cling.
They giggle, wobble, turn around,
In every secret, joy is found.

Time's Tasting Room

Sip the laughter, spill the cheer,
A taste of joy, oh so near!
With laughter bubbles, we can see,
Time's best vintage sets us free.

Every sip a fleeting joke,
As giggling vines begin to croak.
Glasses raised to every blunder,
In this room, we laugh like thunder.

A Palette of Dusk and Dew

Brush the dew on cheeks so round,
With every splash, new giggles found.
Dusk paints colors wild and bright,
Where every shadow sparks delight.

Wine spills over in playful arcs,
Tickling vines with joyful sparks.
A palette formed by whimsy's hand,
Crafting laughter across the land.

Sip of Nostalgia

A sip from the past brings a grin,
Memories bubbling like a cheeky gin.
Conversations swirl like dandelion seeds,
Uncorking laughter, that's all that one needs.

Oh, the time when we danced in our socks,
Chasing our shadows, playing with clocks.
Now we sip slowly, and chuckle at fate,
Realizing childhood was often just great!

Clusters of Contemplation

In clusters we gather, ideas may clash,
Like grapes on the vine, we sometimes must thrash.
Philosophies bounce off each other's head,
Who knew these thoughts could lead us to dread?

Jokes round the table, our minds start to spin,
What if the world is just one big din?
The laughter is rich, with a fruity bouquet,
At least it's a free show, we'll take it today!

The Wine of Wisdom

Pour me a glass of the wise and the witty,
A blend that's so smooth, it's just a bit gritty.
With each tiny sip, let the wisdom flow,
Just don't drink it fast, or you'll start to glow!

Old tales are aged, like cheese and like wine,
They sometimes taste funny, but they'll be just fine.
So here's to the moments we take with a cheer,
Raise a glass to the past, laughter's always near!

Uncorking the Past

Uncorking the past is a curious deed,
You never quite know what's lurking, indeed.
Is it sweet like a dream, or sharp as a dart?
Some memories sparkle, while others just dart.

From silly escapades to the times we were bold,
Each story unfolds like a tale to be told.
With laughter we pry at the bottles, we find,
That life's bubbling mystery is one of a kind!

Lament of Dried Leaves

In the autumn breeze, they twirl and spin,
Like gossiping friends, they lose their skin.
Once thriving in green, now brittle and brown,
They crack and crumble, a sad leafy gown.

Leaves whisper secrets of seasons gone by,
Underneath the moon, they shiver and sigh.
"Why must we fade?" they ask with a groan,
As they dance with the wind, feeling quite alone.

Through the Cellar Door

A creaky old door leads to what lies below,
With barrels of dreams and a hint of a glow.
Dust bunnies waltz on the floor with great flair,
While bottles above pray, 'Please don't despair!'

The shadows are friends with stories to tell,
Of boozy blunders and a tipsy farewell.
As corks pop like fireworks, laughter erupts,
In this merry chaos, all seriousness is trumped.

Past and Present Palate

A sip from the past, a gulp of delight,
With flavors so bold, they'll give you a fright.
The fruit of the vine, it chuckles and jokes,
As memories swirl with mischievous pokes.

In this mixing pot of a fine vintage blend,
The present gets tipsy; the past is a friend.
With laughter and bubbles, they toast and they cheer,
"Here's to the sips that brought us right here!"

The Legacy of Liquid Sunshine

A bottle of sunshine, so bright and so bold,
With stories of harvest and laughter retold.
Each drop pours a giggle, a tickle in time,
As memories bubble in rhythm and rhyme.

Liquid gold flows with wit in each sip,
Transporting poor souls on a whimsical trip.
The world gets a chuckle, a wink, and a cheer,
In this legacy bright, no gloom can come near.

Vines of Solitude

In a garden of quiet, I sat in a chair,
Watching the plants grow, like they just didn't care.
A snail on a mission, moving so slow,
He winked at the vines, said, 'Come on, let's go!'

The weeds had a party, they danced in a row,
Rooting for freedom, with nowhere to sow.
The sun held a picnic with clouds in the sky,
While I sipped my lemonade, letting out a sigh.

Bunches of Insight

I pondered my snacks while munching on bread,
Deciding my future, or so it was said.
A grape rolled away, it slipped on the floor,
It giggled at me, and then rolled out the door!

With wise little colors, the fruits shared their dreams,
A banana chimed in, 'Life's better with creams!'
I laughed at their antics, forgot all my woes,
As I piled up my thoughts like new winter clothes.

The Crush of Reminiscence

An old bottle lurked, with dust on the top,
Promising stories, the memories pop.
I poured out some laughter, mixed in a jest,
A toast to the moments that turned to a fest!

The cork made a joke, said, 'I'm feeling so fine!'
As bubbles of laughter rose up like a vine.
We drank to the memories, the silly, the sweet,
In this crush of recall, life's absurdity's neat.

A Palette of Emotions

With colors and hues, I painted my day,
A canvas of giggles, in the sun's bright ray.
The greens laughed at yellows, what a vibrant affair,
While blues rolled their eyes, trying hard to not care!

The reds blushed with laughter, swirling around,
As purples danced giddily, not making a sound.
In this mix of madness, no brush quite so straight,
We twirled through the colors, loving our fate.

Sipping the Past

A glass of memories spills around,
Each sip a story, lost but found.
Laughs emerge from shadows cast,
As we toast the goofiness of the past.

Time wrinkles without a care,
We reminisce in comfy chairs.
Each chuckle a ticking clock,
Nose to the glass, we laugh and mock.

Oh, those blunders we adore,
Missteps that leave us wanting more.
With every sip, the grin extends,
Forty years but still like friends.

In youth's embrace, we danced with flair,
Now we wobble, but we don't despair.
Raise your glass and let's make a fuss,
For time may bend, but laughter's a plus.

Dusk's Tasting Board

As twilight spreads its funny cloak,
We gather 'round, and someone spoke.
The snacks are odd, the drinks absurd,
With each new taste, we feel a blurred.

Pickled grapes and cheese so strong,
Who knew they'd ever get along?
We munch and sip, giggles in piles,
What's that flavor? A hint of wiles!

A salad dressed in silly chats,
Where laughter dances like curious cats.
A toast to oddities on this board,
Who knew life could be such a hoard?

But as the sunset brings a grin,
We cheer to flavors, we dive right in.
Dusk's tasting board, a splendid cheer,
A feast for laughter, we end the year.

The Yearning of Ripe Bunches

In orchards ripe with dreams so bold,
Bunches dangle, stories untold.
Each cluster hangs with a cheeky tease,
Craving the laughter, if you please!

We tiptoe lightly on the vine,
With every step, the grapes align.
Who knew that flavor could bring such fun?
In search of sweetness, we're never done!

Ripe bunches sway and call our name,
Each bite, a taste of silly fame.
We pluck the joy, a joyful fight,
With each round bite, we dance in light.

So here we are, with juice on our face,
In moments of laughter, we find our place.
As ripe bundles jive in the summer's sun,
Yearning for laughter has just begun.

Echoes of Twilight

Dusk whispers softly, tales on the breeze,
As shadows dance with a wink in the trees.
We gather 'round with cups raised high,
At twilight's echo, we laugh and sigh.

The moon is a joker in the starry night,
Shining down on our giddy delight.
With every call from the nighttime crew,
We join in the fun, just me and you.

Missteps are magic, clumsiness divine,
With echoes of laughter, we taste the wine.
So drink up the moments, let giggles arise,
In twilight's embrace, we'll savor the skies.

As stars twinkle secrets, we share goofy tales,
In echoes of twilight, joy never fails.
For laughter, dear friend, is the sweetest refrain,
As the night whispers softly, we'll do it again.

The Aroma of Days Forgotten

In the cellar of memory, dust gathers tight,
Whispers of laughter waft through the night.
Yesterday's snacks, a peculiar delight,
Pickled cucumber, my late-night bite.

Jars filled with sunshine, preserved with a grin,
Chutneys and sauces where chaos begins.
Old recipes scribbled with questionable kin,
Sipping on nostalgia, let the feast begin!

Sun-kissed Reminders

Golden rays dance on our topsy-turvy hats,
Remember the times we rolled like acrobats?
Sunburnt giggles and sandy spats,
Chasing the ice cream truck, oh, how it chats!

Days of chaos, with lemonade spills,
Stumbling through gardens with quirky thrills.
Sunset romances and silly drills,
Reminded by laughter, life just fills!

The Barrels of our Yesterdays

Barrels of laughter, aged like fine cheese,
Cracking old jokes in the summer breeze.
Sipping sweet memories, just like bees,
Buzzing around tales that never cease.

Rolling through vineyards of youthful schemes,
Tasting our fails like forgotten dreams.
Grappling with gaffes and whimsical themes,
Cheers to the follies wrapped in moonbeams!

Symphony of the Season's End

As leaves pirouette in a gusty refrain,
We dance with our shadows, not caring for rain.
With raucous roustabouts, no time to feign,
Sipping on soup that was once a fine grain.

The finale of summer, a sweet serenade,
Chasing our follies with joy unafraid.
An orchestra hums as mistakes are displayed,
In the grand hall of laughter, memories are laid!

Twisted Roots of Thought

In a vineyard of bumbles, I twist and I twine,
Thoughts like grapes tumble, oh, isn't that fine?
I ponder the chaos, I laugh at the mess,
With vines wrapped in nonsense, I must confess.

Each vine tells a story, a gaff or a laugh,
As I dance with my shadows, we share a good graph.
The roots, they are tangled, but oh what a sight,
I toast to confusion, it feels just so right.

With each juicy folly, my worries unwind,
A sip from adventure, it's bliss I can find.
So let's raise a mug, filled with thought's finest wine,
And chuckle at wisdom, both silly and divine.

In the Cellar of Dreams

Deep in my cellar, where dreams often stew,
I found a corked bottle, of thoughts slightly askew.
With a pop and a fizz, they spilled on the floor,
And danced like a dance troupe, then begged for encore.

The shelves were all crowded with hopes and with schemes,
Some sweet like a sundae, or bursting with dreams.
I tasted the laughter, it tickled my tongue,
In the cellar of whimsy, forever I'm young.

So let's drink to the mishaps, the hiccups of fate,
For each silly moment, I simply can't wait.
The cellar is stocked with delight in a jar,
With bubbles of joy, we'll laugh from afar.

Vintage Echoes

In the corners of time, vintage echoes reside,
Whispering secrets of foolish pride.
The laughter erupts from old barrels so wise,
As tales of my blunders twinkle in my eyes.

With sips of nostalgia, I giggle and cheer,
Each echo a riddle, a reminder, my dear.
The cork always pops with memories so bright,
In laughter's embrace, everything feels right.

So gather around, friends, for stories to share,
Of missteps and mishaps, there's plenty of flair.
We'll raise our old glasses to moments that shine,
With vintage echoes, let's drink up the wine!

Tasting the Days Gone By

With a fork full of moments, I feast on the past,
There's joy in my platter, and giggles amassed.
Each bite tastes of sunshine, each glass gleams with cheer,

Oh, tasting the days gone by, it's perfectly clear.

From disasters so silly to victories grand,
I savor the flavors, a buffet just so planned.
Life's banquet is scrumptious, I'll take another slice,
For laughter is ketchup, and regret's just the spice.

So join in the banquet, let's lift up our plates,
To memories tangy and delightful debates.
With a toast to the days, we shall always comply,
In tasting adventures, we'll always get by.

Harvesting Hues of Tomorrow

In fields of gold, we skip and sway,
With baskets full, we dance and play.
The fruit so fine, a sight to see,
We'll whine and dine, just wait for me!

The sun is shining, we laugh, we cheer,
Collecting colors, let's toast with beer!
Our puns are ripe, our jokes all spry,
In a bustling grove, oh me, oh my!

A purple laugh, a green delight,
Our shady tales take flight tonight.
The vines are gossiping, branches bend,
As we sip our juice and make new friends.

We stash them away in jars so bright,
And hope they don't give us a fright.
In dreams, we sip on giggles, cheers!
Tomorrow's harvest brings new cheers!

Reflections in a Wineglass

A swirl of giggles fills the cup,
As dreams and puns begin to sup.
I spy my face through Merlot's glare,
Am I a genius or just a hare?

Flip my glass, watch laughter pour,
Each sip reveals a tale of yore.
Is that a wink or just the wine?
A chuckle bubbles, oh, how divine!

With friends we toast to fleeting fads,
As we swirl around with playful jabs.
Each clink resounds like a hearty cheer,
Who knew reflections could taste so dear?

The remnants dance on the table bright,
Leaving behind a giggling sight.
As we raise our glasses high in jest,
In a world of sips, we feel the best!

Bottled Echoes of Summer

Under the sun, we chase a breeze,
With laughter mixed like honeyed tease.
Bottles clink with a fizzy roar,
As echoes play like kids galore.

The laughter bubbles, a fizzy blend,
Each sip, a story, without an end.
Did I just taste a hint of cheese?
Or was that last sip just car keys, please?

We share our tales, the funny kind,
With each reflection, our joys unwind.
Sipping slow, we're lost in rhyme,
Let's bottle up this giggly time!

As dusk settles, the sky a ruby,
We toast to nights so warm and pubby.
In every bottle, our laughter glows,
Like summer echoes, how our friendship grows!

The Savoring Silence

At dusk, we pause, no words to share,
In the quiet glow of fragrant air.
A sip of bliss, a silent joke,
In tasseled twilight, time we'll stoke.

With every sip, we rise and hover,
Like bees who forget, oh brother, oh lover!
A nod, a grin, the night wraps tight,
Our hearts echo softly, a cozy light.

We hide our laughter in strawberry mints,
With every delay, our patience hints.
In savoring silence, we find the gold,
In a hush of joy, such stories told.

So let's sip slow in this tranquil trance,
Where every moment offers a chance.
With a clink of glasses, here we remain,
In the savoring silence, our joy's unchained!

Harvest of Memories

In the cellar, laughter spills,
Old corks popping give us thrills.
Bottles roll with wobbling glee,
Each sip's a toast to memory!

Squished toes turn to grape juice flow,
A squabble starts, who gets to go?
We'll stomp and dance, a squishy mess,
This winemaking's a funny quest!

Jugs of laughter fill the air,
As friends all stumble without care.
We'll raise our glasses, toast with cheer,
For every laugh, we hold so dear!

So here's to nights beneath the moon,
With laughter's echo like a tune.
When memories age, they sweetly swell,
In this funny grape-filled carousel!

Echoes in the Vineyard

Beneath the leaves, we skedaddle,
Chasing squirrels, it's quite the battle.
Old vines creak, whispering jokes,
As we roam, those silly folks!

"Who stomped my foot?" we shout in jest,
The squirrels giggle, never rest.
With squished grapes and muddy knees,
We sip our wine with clownish ease!

Sipping vineyards, what a sight,
Asgrowing grapes hold tales of light.
With every laugh, a memory clings,
Amidst the chaos, the joy it brings!

Oh, echoes of laughter in the breeze,
As we dance 'round like buzzing bees.
With every sip, the stories blend,
In this funny vine-draped trend!

Reflections Beneath the Vines

Underneath our favorite vine,
We tell our tales, both yours and mine.
With chuckles bubbling from our lips,
We dream of vineyards filled with quips!

Wobbling glasses, tipsy spills,
Our laughter echoes through the hills.
We ponder life, while sipping slow,
Each grape holds secrets, don't you know?

In dappled shade, we play a game,
Of silly songs, no one's the same.
The grape v. foot race is on,
Let's see who wins before it's dawn!

As daylight fades, the stories grow,
With every laugh, our spirits glow.
Beneath the vines, where joy entwines,
We find the magic in the signs!

Whispers of Sweetness

In the orchard, riotous delight,
Where grapes wear smiles, oh so bright!
A slip on skins, a giggle's chase,
With friends all scattered in this space!

Bubbling juice and silly cheers,
We toast to all our goofy years.
A grape fight starts, what a grand show,
Sweetness wrapped in laughter's glow!

As dusk approaches, stories weave,
Every vine knows the tricks we leave.
With sweetness draped, we twirl and sway,
In this world, it's fun all day!

So let's rejoice 'neath the starry skies,
With whispered secrets in our eyes.
For in this vineyard, life's complete,
With every laugh, we stomp our feet!

Memories in the Mellowed Glass

In a glass so round, I see,
Dancing grapes that talk to me.
They giggle as they swirl around,
In this party, joy is found.

The cork pops loud, it's quite a scene,
As I toast to a life unseen.
With bubbles rising, laughter flows,
What a show, the fun just grows!

Each sip a trip down memory lane,
Where silliness can never wane.
Those moments saved in shades so bright,
Turned quirky in this wine's soft light.

So here's to time, both sweet and bold,
In every drop, new tales are told.
It's all a bit of silly fun,
In this glass, we're all as one.

Harvest's Quiet Rebellion

The harvest sings a silly tune,
Beneath the lazy afternoon.
Grapes in carts, they play a game,
Charging forth without a name.

Each bunch decides to take a break,
Rolling 'round, oh what a shake!
They giggle loud in juicy glee,
A raucous bunch—oh let them be!

The farmers pause, shake their heads,
As grapes plan mischief from their beds.
The bins are castles, ripe with spite,
In this playground, what a sight!

Boundless grapes slight every toil,
In laughter's dance, the tensions boil.
So here's to chaos in the field,
Where juicy fruits refuse to yield.

Reflections in Unfermented Clouds

Above the vineyards in bright skies,
Fluffy clouds share grape-filled lies.
"Oh look!" they say, "We're all so fine,
Just floating here, no need for wine!"

The grapes beneath let out a cheer,
"Oh clouds, you're fuzzy little dear!"
They bounce around, quite full of cheer,
While clouds just float, not wanting beer.

With every squish that meets the ground,
The laughter echoes all around.
It seems the sky knows how to play,
While grapes get squishy day by day.

So as the sun shines bright and bold,
Even clouds can't resist the fold.
With giggles shared between the hues,
It's all a comedy of grape views.

A Sip of Serenity

A sip so sweet, a laugh bestowed,
In every gulp, a story flowed.
I swirled it round with such delight,
What mischief lurked in this soft night?

The glass held jokes that stole my breath,
In every drop, a little death.
For swirling thoughts, they kindly drown,
In fruity fun, I spin around.

A sip brings peace, a silly grin,
As laughter bursts from deep within.
Here's to the moments sweet and silly,
Potato chip crumbs make it silly-dilly!

So raise your glass, don't hold it back,
With every clink, the joy we pack.
In the quiet murmur of night's embrace,
We find our laughter in this place.

Veils of Memory

In the orchard of my youth,
Where laughter danced with the dew,
I tripped on roots of wisdom,
And fell into a dream or two.

Those days a swirl of silly pranks,
With whispers among vine-clad banks,
I swore I'd never poke that bee,
Yet he and I had quite the spree!

Now memories hang like ripe old fruit,
Some sweet, some sour, oh what a hoot!
With every bite, a story spills,
Like juice that drips on window sills.

As I recall those sunlit hours,
I'm left with drunken thoughts like flowers,
They bloom with quirks, a playful jest,
And leave me giggling, feeling blessed.

Fruitful Soliloquies

Beneath a tree of age and charm,
I found some thoughts that work like balm,
Each fruit a giggle, ripe and round,
With seeds of wisdom underground.

I spoke to pears, they rolled their eyes,
While apples chuckled, full of lies,
A banana slipped on all the fun,
Declaring clearly, 'We're not done!'

With every slice of juicy chat,
Philosophy dressed in a silly hat,
The oranges chimed with citrus cheer,
Crowning the day with laughter near.

So here I stand, with fruit in hand,
Each laugh a seed, a well-planned strand,
My revelries in nature's grin,
A fruitful solo where jokes begin.

Trellis of Thought

Up high upon a wooden frame,
My thoughts are climbing just the same,
Like grapes with laughter in the breeze,
They twist and turn with silly ease.

Each thought a cluster, ripe and clear,
With juicy tales that make me cheer,
I wrangle words as vines entwine,
Creating jests like aged fine wine.

So here I tangle, laugh and spin,
With witticisms tucked within,
My trellis wrapped with glee and mirth,
Each memory shows its playful worth.

A summit of giggles, I shall glean,
As every leaf whispers, 'What a scene!'
So let the laughter take its flight,
On this trellis, the world feels bright.

The Pomegranate's Truth

In the market where colors bloom,
Lies a fruit known to cause a zoom,
A pomegranate bursting with jest,
Its inner seeds, they love to fest.

I've cracked one open, what a sight!
These little gems are pure delight,
Each bounce and pop a playful tease,
Unraveling laughter with such ease.

They whisper secrets, oh so grand,
Of friendships forged in sunlight's hand,
A scoop of joy in every bite,
Each morsel shares the heart's own light.

So let us gather, laugh and share,
The truths of life, both sweet and rare,
With pomegranate wisdom to impart,
A fruity joke that warms the heart.

Vines of Memory

In the cellar of my mind, I find,
Old bottles with labels, uniquely designed.
Each sip is a laugh, a tale to tell,
Of mishaps and moments, we know all too well.

A vintage mishap, oh what a scene,
Tripped over my cat, spilled wine on my jeans.
Memories dance like grapes on the vine,
Crushing the past, in bubbles we dine.

Picturing friends with glasses in hand,
Belly laughs echo, like waves on the sand.
Life pours out fun, let the corks fly free,
As I stumble upon my own history.

Roots of Time

Roots twist and turn, beneath the ground,
Digging up laughter where joy can be found.
Tickling my toes, they whisper and tease,
"Your time's getting short, don't slouch, bend your knees!"

With each passing year, they dig in so deep,
While I chase the dreams that make me lose sleep.
They remind me of moments, sweet as can be,
Which sprouted up quick like a grape from a tree.

The roots wink at me, say it's all a big joke,
Life's just a comedy, if you merely provoke.
So I dance with my shadows, embrace what I find,
Making wine from my woes, blending heart with the grind.

Uncorked Journeys

Pop the cork, let the laughter out,
Our journeys are wild, there's no doubt.
With grapes on our heads, we waddle and sway,
Life's a big party, come join the array!

We traveled through valleys, we tumbled with glee,
Chasing the sun, much like a bee.
Each trip was a bottle, corked tight with delight,
Uncorking memories, under moonlight so bright.

Fueled by the giggles, we clink our fine glasses,
Sharing our stories, let time slowly passes.
With every new vintage, it only gets better,
So toast to the mischief that bonds us forever!

Maturing Through the Seasons

Seasons roll by, like a wheel in a race,
Growing older and weirder, oh what a place!
Spring brings the giggles, summer's a blast,
Then autumn decides, "Hold your fun fast!"

Winter's a snooze, with cold feet all night,
But with nights by the fire, everything's right.
Life ages like cheese, brave enough to try,
Witty and wise, with a glittering eye.

From green bud to ripe, nature knows best,
Yielding tales full of joy, laughter in jest.
So here's to the whims of old Father Time,
Turning tickles to treasures, in rhythm and rhyme.

A Glass of Yesterday

Raise a glass to the past, so quirky and bright,
With memories swirling, like stars in the night.
Each drop a reminiscence, a sip of delight,
Laughs echo softly, like whispers in flight.

Yesterday's frolics, with friends by my side,
Tales of mishaps and giggles, pour out with pride.
Every toast is a flashback, a stumble, a cheer,
With bubbles of laughter, we lift our good beer.

So sip on the moments, don't let them go stale,
For a good story always has room to regale.
A glass half full, let the enjoyment arise,
In the vineyard of life, where the funny stuff lies.

Diary of a Decaying Cluster

In the cellar I sit and pout,
My friends are all gone, that's without doubt.
Once we were plump, vibrant, and bold,
Now I'm just wrinkled, or so I'm told.

I recall the days of sunshine and cheer,
When every drop of rain brought a beer.
Now I mold with dreams of a vine's sweet song,
Hoping for laughter to keep me strong.

The party's over, the bottles are dry,
I watch the corks pop and wonder why.
They toast and they clink, but where is my share?
Just me and my thoughts, alone in despair.

Reflecting on life as I slowly fade,
Tiny fruit flies now make their parade.
Oh, what a saga of life in a bunch,
Where everything's sweet, then turns to a crunch!

From Grapes to Ghosts

In a vineyard so lush, where the laughter would play,
I stumbled upon the spirits of yesterday.
They whispered of harvests, of late summer sighs,
Now I float through the fields with curious eyes.

These phantoms of flavor, they giggle and glide,
Sharing tales of the grapes they once tried to hide.
'Oh, remember those feasts where we rolled in the sun?'
I chuckle and nod, oh what fun we did run!

Now I'm left to wander in twilight's embrace,
A jester of vines, in this mischievous space.
The spectral grapes chuckle with mischief in mind,
'Join us dear friend, leave your worries behind!'

As I swish through the shadows, I ponder my fate,
The ghostly grapes giggle, 'You're never too late!'
With laughter we're bound, through fermentation we dance,
From sweet little clusters to ghosts in a trance.

Layers of Liquid Light

In a bottle of sunshine, I'm layered with glee,
Each sip of my essence, a taste of the sea.
With bubbles of joy that pop in my glass,
Reflecting the sunlight, oh how the moments pass!

They swirl me with laughter, they swirl me with zest,
Oh, how I shine in my bottled-up vest!
Each pour is a giggle, each sip is a cheer,
Layers of liquid, bringing humans near.

I like to play dress-up, in glasses I prance,
A waltz with the cork, a bubbly romance.
With each birthday toast, I feel like a star,
In this funny old world, I'm a liquid avatar!

So raise up your glasses, let's laugh 'til we drop,
Together we'll spill, maybe even just stop.
For life, dear friend, is a banquet divine,
With layers of laughter, in each drop of wine.

Last Drops of the Season

As autumn's chill blankets the trembling vine,
I watch the last drops collect, oh so fine.
The harvest is over, it's time to retreat,
But look at me laughing, I'm still quite a treat!

The final fruition, a party in hue,
With every last gulp, I'm bidding adieu.
Sipping on sunshine while balancing gloom,
I dance in the glass, in this twilight room.

So fizzle and pop with your friends by the barrel,
Remember the fun, let not joy be a peril.
With giggles and tips, we will surely unite,
As the last drops of season slip into the night.

So let's raise a toast to the sweet fleeting days,
Where laughter and memories flow in wavy ways.
Catch me if you can, in this merry good-bye,
For even in endings, the fun is nearby!

Bubbles in the Bottled Past

In the cellar, I found a cork,
A relic of days, like a quirky dork.
Each bubble a giggle, each fizz a jest,
A laugh with the past, oh what a fest.

Forgotten bottles, their labels askew,
Whispering secrets of times I once knew.
The cork pops loud, like my friends' wild cheer,
We toast to the years filled with giggles and beer.

Recalling the times we danced on the green,
With silly old hats, and faces still keen.
The bubbles, they rise, like the tales of the night,
Each burp brings a memory that feels just right.

So here's to the laughs, and the corks that we pop,
With every sip, I just can't help but stop.
To treasure the moments, both silly and fat,
As I sip on the giggles, and tip my old hat.

Sipping on Memories

I pour out the laughter, a sweet vintage wine,
Each sip brings a memory, dancing in line.
I chuckle and snicker, as I swirl and I taste,
With each playful memory, no time to waste.

The time I wore socks with sandals, so bold,
Reflecting on choices, I gladly retold.
That dress-up party, oh what a sight,
We wore our best jokes like a crown shining bright.

Sipping on memories, I savor the past,
With friends by my side, these moments hold fast.
The stories, like flavors, swirl round in my head,
The laughter, the blunders, the mischief we bred.

So raise a glass high, let the shenanigans flow,
To memories sweet as a ripe summer glow.
For in every sip, I find joy that will last,
As I laugh at the lessons that time's kindly cast.

The Fermentation of Regret

In the barrel of time, I stirred up a brew,
A cocktail of choices, from silly to skew.
The bubbles erupt with each thought that I find,
Regrets on the rocks, but they're one of a kind.

Oh, the days I forgot to wear matching shoes,
Or the haircut I thought was an artistic muse.
Each sip is a lesson, each gulp is a grin,
As I ponder the past, where faux pas begin.

Fermentation? More like a comedy show,
My life's the punchline, and I'm stealing the glow.
With a chuckle I pour, and I take a big swig,
For regrets turn to laughter, oh life's such a gig!

So here's to the blunders and slips that I make,
I'll toast to my folly with each silly mistake.
For in this great brew of what's been and what's yet,
Life's a giggle-filled feast, I'll never forget.

Twisted Roots and Wandering Dreams

Twisted roots hide tales of mischief and fun,
Each branch holds a secret under the sun.
As I wander through moments, both silly and sweet,
I trip over laughter that lifts up my feet.

The trees seem to chuckle with every big swing,
In the shade of their branches, I hear the birds sing.
I dance with the shadows, while sipping a cheer,
Connected to memories, a vine full of cheer.

Wandering dreams converge on paths of the past,
Each turn's like a riddle, a raucous contrast.
With the ticklish breeze whispering soft to my ear,
I give in to giggles, my worries disappear.

So let's laugh with the twirls, and the wiggles of fate,
For the roots that we grow will only translate.
To the funny little stories that sprout day by day,
In the garden of laughter where we choose to play.

A Tapestry of Vintage Dreams

In a vineyard where antics bloom,
Grapes dance lightly, dispelling gloom.
Each vine whispers a giggling tune,
Sunshine giggles beneath the moon.

Bottles chuckle in a clever way,
As corks pop off and start to play.
Sipping sweetness, laughter flows,
Grape must tricks us into prose.

Each drop tells tales of silly times,
Of clumsy feet and clanking chimes.
With vintage flair, we toast with glee,
Cheerful sips of jubilee.

So let us weave this joyous thread,
In every glass, a fun story spread.
From vineyard dreams, let spirits rise,
And share the joy in every size.

Shadows Among the Bunches

Among the rows where shadows play,
Bunches giggle in a sneaky way.
They poke their heads from vines so green,
In friendly banter, they're quite the scene.

A grape proposes a silly game,
While others whisper, 'Let's stake our claim!'
Round and round, the fun begins,
We laugh until we shed our skins.

The shadows chuckle, faint and light,
As we spin tales into the night.
Each grape a player, full of cheer,
In this silly fruit-filled atmosphere.

When it's time to bid adieu,
We hold onto these memories too.
For in the darkness, we found our punch,
Among the shadows, we ate the lunch!

Juices of Time

Oh, the juicy tales they tell,
Of summer days and autumn swell.
A splash of laughter, a swirl of zest,
In every sip, we find our quest.

Sloshing buckets, a bubbly brew,
Straw hats tipped with shades of blue.
A toast to spills and silly crowns,
As grapes tumble down, no need for frowns.

Time is sweet, or so they say,
With every squirt, we dance and sway.
Gleeful aromas waft through the air,
Cultivated chaos, but we don't care!

So let us fill our cups with cheer,
As we share the juice of every year.
Raise your glass, let laughter climb,
Here's to the times we juice with rhyme!

Pondering the Ripened Seasons

In seasons ripe with childish schemes,
We ponder life and all its dreams.
Grapes adorned in purple sheen,
We giggle at what might have been.

From crush to crunch, it's quite absurd,
The hiccup of a laughing bird.
With every grape, a pondered thought,
Of summer fun and battles fought.

The sunshine beams, the shadows laugh,
As we sip our way through grape-staffed life.
Each drop a ponder, light and free,
In life's grand banquet, we find a key.

So raise your glass to vintage schemes,
Where laughter flows like summer streams.
In every sip, we find the reason,
To cherish fun in every season!

When Vines Speak

In the vineyard where laughter grows,
The vines gossip about our prose.
They twist and twirl, a funny sight,
As they debate the day's delight.

They say the sun's a lazy fright,
Too warm to work, just lounging right.
The wind chimes join in with a cheer,
Whispering secrets, far and near.

They joke about the clumsy crow,
Who tripped on roots and stole the show.
And as the flowers burst with glee,
They toast to all their vine-y tea.

So next you pass through leafy lanes,
Remember, laughter flows in veins.
Each cluster's chuckle is quite grand,
If only we could understand!

Celestial Sips

Under stars, the night does shine,
We gather grapes, a twisted line.
A sip of joy from cosmic wells,
Tasting laughter, no need for spells.

The moon joins in with a sly grin,
"Why not let the fun begin?"
A comet flashes, bright and fleet,
While we raise glasses to the beat.

Jovial bubbles dance around,
As stars drop by without a sound.
They poke fun at the sun's big head,
Sipping stardust, til' we're fed.

When laughter turns into delight,
Our hearts are warm, our futures bright.
So let the wine flow like the night,
Cheers to humor, our cosmic rite!

Among Forgotten Grapes

In a cellar where dust does cling,
Forgotten grapes begin to sing.
They reminisce the days of yore,
When every drink opened a door.

They artfully debate their fate,
"Will they become juice or end up late?"
Jokes fly as corkscrews spin away,
Planning parties for the next Monday.

They giggle at their neighbor's plight,
Who in the dark confused day with night.
"I mean, who drinks wine with cereal?"
Pipe the grapes, "Now, that's a serial!"

Among the barrels, laughter grows,
As stories bubble, the humor flows.
Cheers to those who dare to sip,
And share a joke on life's wild trip!

The Solace of Aging Barrels

In the corners where barrels sigh,
Time tickles them with every try.
They share tales of the grapes they held,
Of cheeky sips, and laughs compelled.

"Oh dear, remember that wild night?
When a runaway cork caused a fright?"
They chuckle softly, wood creaking loud,
Aged wisdom wrapped in whispers proud.

With every bump and every shake,
A story's born, a new headache.
No finer wine than one that's spent,
On laughter and good times well-meant.

So here's to barrels, wise and old,
Guarding every laugh, every bold.
Let's pop some corks and let it flow,
For aging well is the way to go!

Notes of Nostalgia

In a land of sunlit vines,
We danced among the grapes,
Forgot our shoes in tangled knots,
And laughed at silly shapes.

The chicken wore a fancy hat,
As we sipped our sweet delight,
Chased by flies with acrobatics,
And giggles through the night.

Old friends grew insane with age,
As memories slipped like wine,
We dribbled stories, spilled some tales,
And feasted on the divine.

The echo of our laugh still rings,
In every vine that bends,
The funny face my cousin made,
Is where the laughter ends.

Lush Memories on the Horizon

Beneath the arching boughs we lay,
With cups full of cheer,
We claimed the world was ours that day,
And shared our silliest fears.

A grape on my head became a hat,
As I posed like a sprite,
My friends took photos, titters loud,
In the golden summer light.

Some danced the cha-cha with old cans,
Thought it the latest groove,
While others held their bellies tight,
And laughed until they moved.

With every sip, the tales grew tall,
Of escapades that spun,
We toasted to the best of times,
While counting grains of fun.

Sunkissed Moments in the Cellar

In a dusty room where secrets sleep,
We cracked open a smile,
With bottles stacked like weary dreams,
We laughed in every aisle.

A cork flew high, a cheeky shot,
The dog leapt up to play,
He found himself on the table,
Dancing like it was May!

The cellar walls shared vintage jokes,
Each bottle told a tale,
Of moments sweetened by our youth,
Where laughter would prevail.

With laughter echoing off the stone,
And sips of something fine,
We spun through time, the past alive,
In every drop of wine.

Vintage Whispers

What stories does the old oak tell?
With roots that dig so deep,
It witnessed our shenanigans,
And all the joy we keep.

A wager made on who could climb,
To snatch the ripest treat,
We tumbled down in tangled limbs,
With laughter loud and sweet.

A jug of juice turned into dreams,
As grass stains marked our knees,
We swayed beneath the starlit skies,
With whispers in the breeze.

Those vintage days may fade away,
Like leaves that softly fall,
Yet in our hearts, they linger on,
A silly, fun-filled call.

Tender Vines and Forgotten Identities

In a vineyard where dreams entwine,
Old bottles laugh, sharing wine's fine line.
Forgotten labels whisper tales that amuse,
Of parties lost and tipsy muse.

Grapes roll around, forming a dance,
While corks pop up, lost in a prance.
Each sip uncovers a jest or surprise,
As vines twist like stories with quirky ties.

In your glass, a joke from years gone by,
With each bubbles burst, let out a sigh.
The past is ripe, yet we can't reclaim,
Those wild identities of grape's fame.

So let's raise a toast to forgotten tries,
To tipsy nights and playful lies.
With laughter shared, let worries unwind,
In the tender vines, joy is defined.

Flavors of Time Uncorked

Pouring memories from a dusty bottle,
Each swirl reveals a time travel throttle.
Cherry giggles mixed with aged despair,
Sip too much and you might start to dare.

With each drop, a funny tale unfolds,
Of misadventures and daring bolds.
Beneath the cork, old friends start to tease,
'Remember when we danced like that breeze?'

A hint of nutmeg from grandma's pie,
Laughter bursts forth; oh, how time can fly!
As flavors collide in a zesty way,
Wine and good humor steal troubles away.

So pop that cork, let the laughter flow,
Time's flavors uncorked, putting on a show.
With each tasty sip, we find our glee,
In moments wrapped in joyous reverie.

The Tantalizing Trace of Tannins

Tannins, oh tannins, what a name!
They dance on the tongue, igniting the game.
With a wink and a swirl, they start to play,
A naughty little flavor leading astray.

In the glass, they tease like a playful ghost,
Whispering secrets, we revel and boast.
"Is it me or is it you?" a friend will say,
An identity crisis in a roundabout way.

The boldest of red can be quite a prank,
With each sip, we lean further on the flank.
Laughter erupts as the chatter starts,
Tannins remind us of funny smarts.

So let's savor the riddle in every pour,
Chasing those laughs while we beg for more.
With every drop, a grin will bloom,
In the tantalizing trace of laughter's room.

Sips of Solitude

In the quiet of night, with a glass in hand,
Sips of solitude, oh so grand.
A chuckle escapes from the darkened sky,
As grapes tease the mind, oh my, oh my!

Sipping slowly, I reminisce alone,
Funny quirks of life in shades overgrown.
A drop spills out, a glance in the air,
The toast to one self, quite beyond compare.

Chardonnay laughs as it slips from the lip,
My inner thoughts drift on this easy trip.
Each bubble a giggle, each swirl a smile,
Finding joy in solitude, just for a while.

Raise your glass to the antics inside,
In sips of solitude, let laughter abide.
Alone but not lonely, the night is bright,
With every sip, the future feels light.

Grapeson the Millstone

Round and round, the grind does go,
Who knew grapes could put on such a show?
They slip and slide, a fruit parade,
In this millstone dance, I've overstayed.

The vintner laughs as juices fly,
"Is it wine or just a fruit pie?"
The squeaks and squabbles echo loud,
Even the grapes might feel too proud.

Oops, there goes another round,
A grape rolls off, hits the ground.
Laughter rings in the warm sun's haze,
As grapes acquire a twist in phase.

A toast to fun on milled delight,
Wine humor brewing, oh what a sight!
With every stomp, a giggly cheer,
Who knew fermentation could be this dear?

Vintner's Reflections

Staring at barrels, the vintner sighs,
"Do grapes ever dream? Guess they're wise!"
Some blend for deep, some for flair,
This one's for giggles, because we dare.

Bottle caps popping like party hats,
Who needs a drink to chat with having chats?
Juggling corks like a circus act,
Laughing till the punchline's unpacked.

Each label tells a story, silly or sweet,
With every taste, we rise to our feet.
"Swirl it, sniff it, what's that you smell?"
Just the scent of giggles, can you tell?

As seasons change, so do the puns,
Chasing after light, the vintner runs.
To sip or not to sip, that is the jest,
In a world of laughter, we're truly blessed.

Glimmers of a Distant Sunrise

At dawn's first light, the grapes awake,
They glance at the sun, a morning quake.
"Is it too bright?" one grape will pout,
"I just want to sleep, let the day be out."

The dew drops dance like a bunch of clowns,
In sunlight's glow, no room for frowns.
With every glimmer, a joke is found,
Some grapes roll on, others just rebound.

"Did you hear? A grape got lost!"
"Don't worry, buddy, you have a cost!"
The laughter spreads, it's a juicy treat,
These morning giggles can't be beat.

So here they bask, in a light-filled cheer,
With bright aspirations, and a hint of beer.
Each sunrise brings frolic and jest,
In the vineyard's embrace, we feel so blessed.

Resounding in Roaring Forties

In the roaring forties, they sing and dance,
Grapes wearing shades in a sunny trance.
"Did I just grape on that floor?" they quip,
"Maybe now I'll take a little trip!"

Each burst of laughter, a grape-ish cheer,
Bounding and bouncing, will you stay here?
The party's wild, fueled by sweet red juice,
A humorous blend, there's no excuse!

Out in the fields, mischief abounds,
Grapes trade jests, they're truly renowned.
"Let's roll with laughter, not just the wine,"
In life's funny moments, we all intertwine.

So raise a glass to the fun-loving crew,
Grapes in the spotlight, with joy to pursue.
In the roaring forties, the sun is bright,
Let's giggle and sip till the day turns right!

www.ingramcontent.com/pod-product-compliance
Lightning Source LLC
Chambersburg PA
CBHW060143230426
43661CB00003B/555